The Little
DESSERT
Cookbook

THE LITTLE
DESSERT
COOKBOOK

SMITHMARK

This edition published in 1996
by Smithmark Publishers,
a division of U.S. Media Holdings, Inc.,
16 East 32nd Street
New York, NY 10016

Smithmark books are available for bulk purchase for sales promotion
and premium use. For details write or call the Manager of Special Sales,
Smithmark Publishers
16 East 32nd Street
New York
NY 10016
(212) 532-6600

© 1996 Anness Publishing Limited

ISBN 0-7651-9817-7

Publisher Joanna Lorenz
Senior Cookery Editor Linda Fraser
Assistant Editor Emma Brown
Designer Patrick McLeavey
Illustrator Anna Koska
Photographers Karl Adamson, Don Last,
James Duncan, Steve Baxter, Amanda Heywood &
Edward Allwright
Recipes Christine France, Carole Clements, Elizabeth Wolf-
Cohen, Carla Capalbo, Sarah Gates, Laura Washburn,
Steven Wheeler, Shirley Gill & Norma MacMillan

Printed in China
10 9 8 7 6 5 4 3 2 1

Contents

Introduction

The strong-willed reach resolutely for the fruit bowl at the conclusion of every meal, but most of us look hopefully at the host or hostess and dream about dessert. Cool and creamy, tart and fruity, or simply sinful, desserts are destined to remain on the menu.

Whatever the weather or season, there's a perfect dessert waiting in the wings, whether it be a comforting Blackberry Cobbler to chase away autumn chill or scoops of Hazelnut Ice Cream to celebrate summer. Friends will flip for Cherry Crêpes and children cheerfully eat their vegetables if a Black Forest Sundae or a slice of gloriously gooey French Chocolate Cake is waiting for them.

When planning a menu, choose a dessert that will complement the preceding courses. A big, hearty casserole calls for a simple sorbet or fruit salad; plainly grilled fish could lead to something really rich and creamy, such as Amaretto Soufflé or Minted Raspberry Bavarois. If you really want to push the boat out and serve a sumptuous sweet such as Hazelnut Meringue Torte with Pears, then keep the rest of the meal as low key as possible.

When serving eight people or more, it is a good idea to offer a choice of desserts. These should contrast in terms of color and content: a fruity Autumn Pudding (a sort of late-harvest summer pudding) with Chocolate Loaf with Coffee Sauce, perhaps. When appropriate, offer a choice of accompaniments, such as yogurt and whipped cream.

For those guests who prefer fresh fruit, take a tip from Thai cuisine. Cut fresh pineapple, melon and papaya into similar-size wedges and overlap them on a decorative platter, with orange and pink grapefruit segments around the rim. Decorate with nasturtiums. Alternately, slice a melon in half, using a zig-zag cut and easing it apart gently. Remove the seeds, then scoop out the flesh with a melon baller. Scrape out any remaining melon, then put the balls back in the half-shell and drizzle with kirsch, Cointreau or Grand Marnier. Add a sprig of mint.

Decorating desserts is approaching an art form. A mousse surrounded by a fresh fruit coulis laced with cream looks exquisite, while rosettes of cream spiked with chocolate leaves would make the perfect topping for a rich mocha mousse. Echo the main ingredient in the dessert, decorating a strawberry cheesecake with chocolate-tipped strawberries or Oranges in Caramel Sauce with strips of orange peel. You can even present a dessert in an edible container, such as when chocolate cups are filled with a liqueur-flavored cream, or impress your guests with Summer Fruit Salad Ice Cream served in an ice bowl that would rival the finest crystal.

This recipe collection ranges from fruity desserts to classic custards, and also includes favorites like Creole Bread and Butter Pudding, Baked Caramel Custard and delicious Cherry Pudding. Choco-holics get a chapter to themselves, and with a White Chocolate Cheesecake, a Chocolate Pavlova and Chocolate Cream Puffs offered, you may be sure everyone will get more than their just desserts!

Ingredients

BUTTER

Use unsalted butter for desserts. Store it in the fridge, in the original wrapper. Freeze unopened sticks in a freezer-proof plastic bag for up to six months.

CHOCOLATE

Most supermarkets stock a good range of chocolate and chocolate products, including sprinkles, chips and syrups. For the best results, use chocolate with a cocoa solid content of at least 50 percent.

CREAM

Half-and-half cream has 18 percent butterfat and is mainly used for pouring into coffee or tea. In whipping cream the butterfat content increases to 35 to 38 percent. desserts decorated with whipped cream should be served on the same day they are made.

EGGS

Unless recipes specify otherwise, use large eggs. Always buy eggs from a reputable supplier, preferably date-stamped, and use them fresh. This is particularly important when the eggs in a recipe are not cooked.

GELATIN

Powdered gelatin is convenient and easy to use. One tablespoon of gelatin is needed for every 2½ cups of liquid. Gelatin must be thoroughly dissolved before use. This is usually done by first softening it in cold water, then heating the mixture gently, stirring constantly. Vegetarian alternatives to gelatin are also widely available

SUGAR

Superfine sugar is used for most desserts, as it dissolves quickly, but granulated sugar is usually preferred for caramel.

8

Decorations

ALMONDS

Thinly sliced almonds, plain or toasted, look good on creamy desserts. Gently press them onto the exposed sides of a frosted cake for a delectable, crunchy coating.

CHOCOLATE CURLS

Pour melted chocolate onto a clean smooth surface, such as a marble slab. When set, draw a broad-bladed cook's knife lightly across the chocolate at an angle of 45°, to cut thin layers that curl into scrolls. The cheater's method is to use a potato peeler on a bar of plain or milk chocolate.

CHOCOLATE LEAVES

Select clean, unblemished, non-poisonous leaves (rose leaves work well) and brush the undersides evenly with melted chocolate. Place on wax paper, refrigerate until set, then carefully peel away the chocolate leaves from the green leaves.

CONFECTIONERS' SUGAR/COCOA POWDER

Lay strips of paper over a dessert before dusting it with confectioners' sugar and/or unsweetened cocoa powder. Carefully remove the paper to give a striped effect.

PIPED CHOCOLATE

Pipe melted chocolate designs on wax paper. Spider webs, hearts and stars all look good, but lift them very carefully when transferring them to a cake or pudding.

WHIPPED CREAM

Swirls, shells and rosettes of whipped cream are easy to make. Use a piping bag fitted with a large, star-shape tip and keep the pressure even. Take care not to overwhip cream for piping – the cream will thicken further as it is forced out of the piping bag. Practice makes perfect – try practicing your piping technique using a cheap alternative to cream, such as instant mashed potatoes!

FRUIT AND FLOWERS

Frosted grapes – made by brushing grapes with water, then dusting them in superfine sugar – look lovely. Fresh rose petals can't be eaten, but look great surrounding a summery sweet. Fruits like strawberries and raspberries make perfect decorations, as do tiny sprigs of red currants.

Techniques

WHIPPING CREAM

Cooks with strong wrists swear that a rotary whisk gives the greatest volume, but a hand-held electric mixer works well. Use heavy or whipping cream for decorations, and be careful not to overwhip the cream. It should just hold its shape and must not look grainy.

MELTING CHOCOLATE

The best way to melt chocolate is over very hot but not boiling water. Break the chocolate into a heat proof bowl. Bring a saucepan of water to a boil, turn off the heat and set the bowl on top. Stir as the chocolate melts. Do not add any liquid to melting chocolate.

FLIPPING A CRÊPE

Crêpes are child's play if you use a good pan, grease it just enough to prevent the batter from sticking, and pour in only enough batter to coat the base evenly. As the crêpe sets, shake the pan to keep it from sticking. Check that it is lightly brown underneath, then hold the pan handle firmly, slide the crêpe forward to the opposite rim and flip it over toward you with a neat flick of your wrist.

WHISKING EGG WHITES

Your bowl and whisk must be clean, dry and completely grease-free. Separate the eggs carefully; if there is any yolk with the whites they will not expand successfully. Beat gently until foamy, then increase the speed and continue whisking until the whites are stiff enough to hold their shape. When adding whisked whites to a stiff mixture, stir in a couple of spoonfuls to lighten it, then fold in the rest.

MAKING CHOCOLATE CUPS

Little chocolate cups make perfect containers for mousses and whips. Use double paper cupcake or candy liners. Using a brush or teaspoon, coat the inside of the liner evenly with melted chocolate, invert, and let set. Peel away the paper and fill just before serving.

PREPARING A SOUFFLE DISH

To make a soufflé which looks as though it has risen above the dish, use a smaller-than-necessary soufflé dish, adding a paper collar to hold the excess mixture in place. Cut a piece of wax paper slightly longer than the circumference of the dish and three times its depth. Fold it over lengthwise, wrap it tightly around the outside of the dish and secure it firmly in place with string or masking tape.

MAKING AN ICE BOWL

Ice creams and sorbets look spectacular in an ice bowl. Choose two freezer-proof bowls, one about 3 inches wider than the other. Pour water into the larger bowl to two-thirds full, then center the small bowl inside it, weighting it so that it floats level with the big bowl. Keep it in place with masking tape. Fill the remaining third with water, then freeze, adding flowers or leaves when the water is semi-frozen. Carefully release the ice bowl once frozen and store in the freezer.

COOK'S TIP

It is not really necessary to make a paper collar for a hot soufflé. Instead, run a clean knife around the edge of the mixture, at a depth of 1/2 inch, to encourage even rising.

Fruit Desserts

Autumn Pudding

INGREDIENTS

10 slices white or whole wheat bread, at least 1 day old
1 Granny Smith apple, peeled, cored and sliced
ripe red plums, halved and pitted
2 cups blackberries
4 tablespoons water
6 tablespoons superfine sugar
yogurt or ricotta cheese, to serve

SERVES 6

13

1 Slice off the crusts from the bread and use a cookie cutter to cut out a 3-inch round from one slice. Cut all the remaining slices in half.

2 Put the bread circle in the base of a 5-cup heat proof baking dish, then overlap the halves around the sides, saving some for the top.

3 Place the fruit, water and sugar in a pan, heat gently until the sugar dissolves, then simmer for 10 minutes, until soft. Drain, reserving the juice.

4 Spoon the fruit into the dish. Top with the reserved bread and juice.

5 Cover the dish with a saucer and place a weight on top of it. Chill the pudding overnight. Turn out onto a serving plate and serve with yogurt.

Cherry Crêpes

INGREDIENTS

CRÊPES
½ cup unbleached all-purpose flour
½ cup whole wheat flour
pinch of salt
1 egg white
⅔ cup milk
⅔ cup water
a little oil, for frying
ricotta cheese, to serve
FILLING
15-ounce can black cherries in juice
1½ teaspoons arrowroot

SERVES 4

1 Sift the flours and salt into a bowl.

2 Make a well in the center of the flour and add the egg white. Gradually beat in the milk and water, whisking hard until all the flour and liquid is incorporated and the batter is smooth and bubbly.

3 Heat a non-stick pan with a small amount of oil until it is very hot. Pour in just enough batter to cover the base of the pan and swirl to cover it evenly.

4 Cook until the crêpe is set and golden, and then turn to cook the other side. Remove to a paper towel and repeat with the remaining batter, to make about eight crêpes in all.

5 Drain the cherries, reserving the juice. Blend about 2 tablespoons of the juice from the can of cherries with the arrowroot in a saucepan. Stir in the rest of the juice. Heat gently, stirring, until boiling. Stir the mixture over medium heat for about 2 minutes, until thickened and clear.

6 Add the cherries to the pan and stir until heated through. Spoon the cherry mixture into the crêpes, fold them in quarters and serve with ricotta cheese.

Poached Pears in Maple-Yogurt Sauce

16

INGREDIENTS

6 firm Anjou pears
1 tablespoon lemon juice
1 cup sweet white wine
thinly pared zest of 1 lemon
1 cinnamon stick
2 tablespoons maple syrup
½ teaspoon arrowroot
⅔ cup plain yogurt

SERVES 6

1 Thinly peel the pears, leaving them whole and with the stalks on. Brush with lemon juice, to prevent them from browning. Using a potato peeler or small knife, scoop out the core from the base of each pear and discard it.

2 Place the pears in a wide, heavy saucepan and add the wine, along with enough cold water to almost cover the pears.

3 Add the lemon zest and cinnamon stick, then bring to a boil. Reduce the heat, cover the pan and simmer for about 30–40 minutes, or until all the pears are

tender. Turn them occasionally so that they cook evenly. Lift out the pears carefully, with a large spoon, draining them well.

4 Bring the remaining liquid to a boil. Boil, uncovered, to reduce to about ½ cup. Strain, and add the maple syrup. Blend some of the liquid with the arrowroot. Return to the pan and cook, stirring, until thick and clear. Cool.

5 Slice each pear about three-quarters of the way through, leaving the slices attached at the stem end. Fan out each pear on a serving plate.

6 Stir 2 tablespoons of the cooled syrup into the plain yogurt and spoon it around each pear on the plates. Drizzle with the remaining syrup and serve the pears immediately.

Oranges in Caramel Sauce

INGREDIENTS

6 large seedless oranges
½ cup granulated sugar

SERVES 6

1 Using a vegetable peeler, remove wide strips of rind from two of the oranges. Stack two or three strips on top of each other and cut them into very thin julienne strips.

2 Cut a slice from the top and the base of each orange. Cut off the peel in strips from the top to the base, following the contours of the fruit.

3 Using a sharp vegetable knife, slice all the peeled fruit crossways into circles about ½ inch thick. Put the orange slices in a serving bowl and cover them with any leftover juice.

4 Fill a large bowl halfway with cold water and set aside. Place the sugar and 3 tablespoons of water in a small heavy pan without a non-stick coating. Bring it to a boil over high heat, swirling the pan to dissolve all the sugar. Boil, without stirring, until the mixture turns a dark caramel color. Remove the pan from the heat and, standing a safe distance back, dip the base of the pan into the bowl of cold water in order to stop the cooking process.

5 Add 2 tablespoons water to the caramel, pouring it down the sides of the pan, and swirling it to mix it thoroughly. Add the strips of orange rind and return the pan to the heat. Simmer over medium-low heat for 8–10 minutes until the orange strips are slightly translucent, stirring occasionally.

6 Pour the caramel and rind over the orange slices in the serving bowl, turn gently to mix everything together and chill for at least 1 hour before serving.

Apples & Raspberries in Rose Tea Syrup

INGREDIENTS

1 teaspoon rose tea
1 teaspoon rose water (optional)
¼ cup granulated sugar
1 teaspoon lemon juice
5 apples
1 cup fresh raspberries

SERVES 4

18

1 Make the tea using 3¾ cups of boiling water together with the rose water, if using. Let steep for 4 minutes.

2 Place the sugar and lemon juice in a large stainless steel saucepan. Carefully strain in all the infused rose tea and stir well until the sugar dissolves.

3 Peel, core and quarter the apples. Poach them in the syrup for about 5 minutes, then transfer the apples and syrup to a large baking sheet and let cool.

4 Pour the cooled apples and rose syrup into a mixing bowl and add the fresh raspberries. Mix well to combine all the ingredients, then spoon the fruit

mixture into individual serving dishes or bowls and serve at room temperature.

COOK'S TIP
If fresh raspberries are out of season, use the same weight of frozen fruit or one 14-ounce can fruit, drained well.

Fresh Fruit with Mango Sauce

INGREDIENTS

1 large ripe mango, peeled, pitted and cubed
rind of 1 orange
juice of 3 oranges
superfine sugar, to taste
2 peaches
2 nectarines
1 small mango, peeled
2 plums
1 pear or ½ small melon
juice of 1 lemon
¼ cup wild strawberries
¼ cup raspberries
¼ cup blueberries
small mint sprigs, to decorate

SERVES 6

I In a food processor fitted with a metal blade, process the large mango until smooth. Add the orange rind, juice and sugar to taste and process again until very smooth. Press through a strainer into a bowl. Chill the sauce until needed.

2 Peel the peaches, then pit and slice the peaches, nectarines, small mango and plums. Peel and quarter the pear, if using, and remove the core. Alternately, seed and slice the half melon thinly and remove all the peel.

3 Place all the sliced fruits on a large plate and sprinkle with the lemon juice to prevent them from discoloring. Chill the plate of fruit, covered with clear plastic wrap, for up to 3 hours before serving.

4 To serve the fruit, arrange the slices on individual serving plates and spoon the strawberries, raspberries and blueberries over the top. Drizzle with a little of the fresh mango sauce and decorate the plates with mint sprigs. Serve the remaining mango sauce separately.

Jellies & Ices

Rhubarb & Orange Granita

1 Trim the rhubarb and slice it into 1-inch lengths. Place it in a pan.

2 Finely grate the rind from the orange and squeeze out all the juice. Add all the rind and about half the orange juice to the rhubarb in the pan and allow to sim-

mer until the rhubarb becomes just tender. Stir in the honey until completely dissolved.

3 Heat the remaining orange juice and stir in the gelatin to dissolve it. Stir it into the rhubarb. Pour the whole mixture into a shallow pan and freeze it for about 2 hours until slushy.

4 Take the mixture out of the freezer and beat it with an electric mixer to break up all the ice crystals. Return the granita to the freezer and freeze until firm. Leave

the granita to soften slightly at room temperature before serving, decorated with orange slices.

INGREDIENTS

12 ounces rhubarb
1 orange
1 tablespoon honey
1 teaspoon powdered gelatin
orange slices, to decorate

SERVES 4

Black Forest Sundae

INGREDIENTS

1 can (14 ounces) cherries in syrup
1 tablespoon cornstarch
3 tablespoons kirsch
2/3 cup whipping cream
1 tablespoon confectioners' sugar
2½ cups chocolate ice cream
4 slices of chocolate cake
8 fresh cherries, to decorate

SERVES 4

24

4 Place a spoonful of the cooled cherries in the bottom of four sundae glasses, then continue with layers of ice cream, chocolate cake, whipped cream and more cherries until the glasses are full.

5 Finish each glass with a piece of chocolate cake, two scoops of ice cream and more whipped cream. Decorate with the fresh cherries.

1 Strain all but 2 tablespoons of the cherry syrup into a saucepan. Measure the cornstarch into a small bowl, add all the remaining syrup and mix well.

2 Bring the syrup in the saucepan to a boil. Stir in the cornstarch and syrup mixture and simmer briefly to thicken. Add the cherries, stir in the kirsch and spread on a baking sheet to cool.

3 Using an electric mixer, whip the cream with the confectioners' sugar until firm.

Hazelnut Ice Cream

1 Spread the hazelnuts on a baking sheet, and toast in a 350°F oven for 3–5 minutes, shaking the sheet frequently. Remove and cool, then place on a clean dish towel, and rub to remove the outer skins. Chop finely, or grind in a food processor with 2 tablespoons of the sugar.

2 Heat the milk in a small pan with the vanilla pod until small bubbles appear on the surface. Remove the pan from the heat. Beat the egg yolks with a wire whisk or electric mixer. Gradually beat in the remaining sugar, and beat for about 5 minutes more until the mixture is pale yellow. Gradually strain in the vanilla milk, discarding the vanilla pod. Stir constantly until all the milk has been added.

3 Pour the mixture into the top of a double boiler, or into a bowl placed over a pan of simmering water. Add the nuts. Stir over medium heat until the water in the bottom pan is  boiling and the custard thickens enough to coat the back of a spoon lightly. Remove from the heat and allow to cool to room temperature. Then refrigerate it, loosely covered, until chilled, a minimum of three hours.

4 Freeze in an ice-cream maker according to manufacturer's directions.

INGREDIENTS

½ cup hazelnuts
6 tablespoons granulated sugar
2 cups milk
4-inch piece of vanilla pod
4 egg yolks

SERVES 4–6

Frozen Apple & Blackberry Terrine

INGREDIENTS

1 pound cooking or eating apples
1 ¼ cups hard cider
1 tablespoon honey
1 teaspoon vanilla extract
*2 cups fresh or frozen and
thawed blackberries*
1 package powdered gelatin
2 egg whites
fresh apple slices and blackberries, to garnish

SERVES 6

1 Peel, core and chop the apples and place them in a pan, with half the cider. Bring the cider to a boil, then cover the pan and let the apples simmer gently until tender.

2 Pour the apples into a food processor or blender and process them to a smooth purée. Stir in the honey and vanilla. Add half the blackberries to half of the apple purée, and then process again until smooth. Strain to remove the seeds.

3 Heat the remaining cider until almost boiling, then add the powdered gelatin and stir until it has completely dissolved. Add half the cider and gelatin to the plain apple purée and the other half to the blackberry and apple purée.

4 Leave the purées to cool until almost set. Whisk the egg whites until they are stiff. Quickly fold them into the apple purée. Remove half of this purée  to another bowl. Stir the remaining whole blackberries into the rest of the apple purée, then pour this into an 8-cup loaf pan and spread it evenly.

5 Top with the blackberry purée and spread it evenly. Finally, add the reserved apple purée and smooth it evenly. If necessary, chill each layer in the freezer for 5 minutes before adding the next.

6 Freeze the layered terrine until firm, about two hours. To serve, allow it to stand at room temperature for 20 minutes so that it softens slightly. Turn it out of the loaf pan and, using a sharp knife, cut it into  even slices. Serve the terrine decorated with fresh apple slices and a few fresh blackberries.

Coffee Jellies with Amaretti Cream

INGREDIENTS

6 tablespoons superfine sugar
2 cups strong hot coffee
2-3 tablespoons dark rum or Kahlua
4 teaspoons powdered gelatin
COFFEE AMARETTI CREAM
⅔ cup heavy or whipping cream
1 tablespoon confectioners' sugar, sifted
2-3 teaspoons instant coffee powder
dissolved in 1 tablespoon hot water
6 large amaretti cookies, crushed

SERVES 4

28

1 Put the sugar in a saucepan with 5 tablespoons of water and stir over gentle heat until dissolved. Increase the heat; allow the syrup to boil steadily, without stirring, for 3–4 minutes.

2 Stir all the hot coffee and rum or Kahlua into the hot syrup. Sprinkle the powdered gelatin over the top and stir until it dissolves completely.

3 Pour the coffee mixture into four parfait glasses and allow them to cool thoroughly, before placing them in the fridge. Leave the glasses in the fridge for several hours until they are completely set.

4 To make the amaretti cream, lightly whip the cream with the confectioners' sugar until it holds stiff peaks. Stir in the instant coffee, then 2 tablespoons of the crushed amaretti cookies.

5 Remove the jellies from the refrigerator. Spoon a little of the coffee amaretti cream on top of the parfaits. Top with the reserved amaretti cookie crumbs and serve the dessert immediately.

Cool Grape Mousse

INGREDIENTS

1 ½ cups green seedless grapes
2 cups white grape juice
1 packet powdered gelatin
½ cup plain yogurt

SERVES 4

1 Reserve four small sprigs of grapes for decoration and then cut the rest in half.

2 Divide the grapes between four stemmed glasses and tilt the glasses to one side, propping them firmly in a bowl of ice.

3 Place the grape juice in a saucepan and heat it until almost boiling. Remove the pan from the heat and add the gelatin, stirring until it dissolves.

4 Pour half the grape juice over the grapes in the tilted glasses and allow to set.

5 Cool the remaining grape juice slightly, then stir it into the yogurt.

6 Stand the four set glasses upright and divide the yogurt mixture among them. Chill until set, about two hours, then top each one with a sprig of grapes before serving.

29

Summer Fruit Salad Ice Cream

INGREDIENTS

7 cups mixed berries, such as raspberries,
strawberries and blueberries
2 eggs
1 cup plain yogurt
¾ cup grape juice
1 packet powdered gelatin

SERVES 6

30

1 Reserve half the fruit and purée the rest in a food processor or blender, or press it through a strainer to make a smooth purée.

2 Separate the eggs and whisk the yolks and the yogurt into the fruit purée.

3 Heat the grape juice until almost boiling, and then remove from the heat. Sprinkle the powdered gelatin over the juice and stir to dissolve completely.

4 Remove the gelatin mixture from the heat and whisk it into the fruit purée until well combined. Pour the mixture into a freezer-proof container. Freeze the fruit purée until half-frozen and slushy in consistency.

5 Using a hand beater or electric mixer, whisk the egg whites until stiff peaks form. Quickly fold them into the half-frozen ice cream mixture.

6 Return the berry mixture to the freezer and freeze until almost firm. Serve it in scoops on small plates, garnished with the reserved whole berries.

Mousses, Custards & Soufflés

Luxury Mocha Mousse

INGREDIENTS

8 ounces good-quality semisweet chocolate, chopped
4 tablespoons espresso or strong coffee
2 tablespoons butter, cut into pieces
2 tablespoons brandy or rum
3 eggs, separated
pinch of salt
3 tablespoons superfine sugar
½ cup heavy or whipping cream
2 tablespoons Kahlua
chocolate-covered coffee beans, to garnish (optional)

SERVES 6

1 In a saucepan over medium heat, melt the chocolate in the coffee, stirring frequently until smooth. Remove from the heat and beat in the butter and brandy or rum.

2 In a small bowl, beat the egg yolks lightly, then whisk in the melted chocolate; the mixture will thicken. Set aside to cool. In a large bowl, beat the egg whites  with an electric mixer. Add a pinch of salt and beat on medium speed until soft peaks form. Increase the speed and beat until stiff peaks form. Beat in the sugar, 1 tablespoon at a time, beating well after each addition until the egg whites are glossy and stiff.

3 Mix a large spoonful of whites into the chocolate mixture to lighten it, then fold the chocolate into the remaining whites. Spoon into 6 individual dishes or a large glass serving bowl and chill for at least 3–4 hours, until set, before serving.

4 In a medium bowl, beat the cream and Kahlua until soft peaks form. Spoon into an icing bag fitted with a medium star tip and pipe rosettes or shells on top of the mousse. Decorate with chocolate-covered coffee beans, if using.

Baked Caramel Custard

INGREDIENTS

1¼ cups sugar
4 tablespoons water
1 vanilla pod
1⅔ cups milk
1 cup heavy or whipping cream
5 large eggs
2 egg yolks

SERVES 6–8

1 Put ¾ cup of the sugar in a small heavy saucepan with the water to moisten. Bring to a boil over high heat, swirling the pan until the sugar dissolves. Boil rapidly, without stirring, until the syrup turns a dark caramel color (this will take about 4–5 minutes).

2 Immediately pour the caramel into a 4-cup soufflé dish. Holding the dish with oven mitts, quickly swirl it to coat the base and sides with the caramel and set aside. (The caramel will harden quickly as it cools.) Place the dish in a small roasting pan. Preheat the oven to 325°F.

3 Split the vanilla pod lengthwise and scrape the black seeds into a saucepan. Add the milk and cream. Bring to a boil over medium-high heat, stirring frequently. Remove the pan from the heat, cover and set aside for 15–20 minutes.

4 In a bowl, whisk the eggs and egg yolks with the remaining sugar for 2–3 minutes until smooth and creamy. Whisk in the hot milk. Strain the mixture into the caramel-lined dish. Cover with foil.

5 Pour enough boiling water into the roasting pan to come halfway up the sides of the dish. Bake the custard for 40–45 minutes until a knife inserted about 2 inches from the edge comes out clean (the custard should be just set). Remove from the roasting pan and cool for at least 30 minutes, then chill overnight.

6 To serve, carefully run a sharp knife around the edge of the dish to loosen the custard. Cover the dish with a plate. Holding them both tightly, invert the dish and plate together. Gently lift one edge of the dish, allowing the caramel to run over the sides, then slowly lift off the dish.

34

Minted Raspberry Bavarois

INGREDIENTS

*3 cups fresh or frozen and
thawed raspberries
2 tablespoons confectioners' sugar
2 tablespoons lemon juice
1 tablespoon finely chopped fresh mint
2 tablespoons powdered gelatin
5 tablespoons boiling water
1¼ cups custard
1¼ cups plain yogurt
fresh mint sprigs, to garnish*

SERVES 6

36

3 Sprinkle 1 teaspoon of the gelatin over 2 tablespoons of boiling water and stir until it has dissolved. Add it to ⅔ cup of the raspberry purée.

4 Pour this jelly into a 4-cup mold, and leave the mold to chill in the fridge until the jelly is just on the point of setting. Tip the mold to swirl the jelly around the sides, then leave to chill until the jelly has set completely.

1 Reserve some raspberries for decoration. Place the rest with the confectioners' sugar and lemon juice in a food processor or blender. Process until smooth.

2 Pass the purée through a strainer to remove the raspberry seeds. Add the chopped fresh mint. You should have about 2½ cups of purée.

5 Stir the rest of the fruit purée into the custard with the yogurt. Dissolve the rest of the gelatin in the rest of the water and stir it into the fruit mixture.

6 Pour the custard into the mold and let chill until it has set. To serve, dip the mold quickly into hot water, then turn it out and decorate it with the reserved raspberries and the mint sprigs.

Baked Custard with Burnt Sugar

INGREDIENTS

1 vanilla pod
4 cups heavy or whipping cream
6 egg yolks
½ cup superfine sugar
2 tablespoons almond or orange liqueur
6 tablespoons light brown sugar

SERVES 6

1 Preheat the oven to 300°F. Place six ½-cup ramekins in a large roasting pan or heat proof dish and set aside.

2 Using a small sharp knife, split the vanilla pod lengthwise and scrape the black seeds into a pan. Add the pod, then add the cream and bring just to a boil over medium-high heat, stirring frequently. Remove from the heat and cover. Set aside for about 15–20 minutes. Remove the vanilla pod.

3 In a bowl, whisk the egg yolks with the superfine sugar and liqueur until well blended. Whisk in the hot cream and strain into a large bowl. Divide among the ramekins.

4 Pour enough boiling water into the roasting pan to come halfway up the sides of the ramekin dishes. Cover the pan with foil and bake for about 30 minutes in the preheated oven until the custards are just set. Remove from the pan and leave to cool. Empty the water from the roasting pan, replace the ramekins and set aside to chill.

5 Preheat the broiler. Sprinkle the light brown sugar evenly over the surface of each custard and broil for 30–60 seconds until the sugar melts and caramelizes. (Do not let the sugar burn or the custard curdle.) Serve immediately.

Amaretto Soufflé

INGREDIENTS

butter, for greasing
½ cup superfine sugar, plus extra
6 amaretti cookies, coarsely crushed
6 tablespoons Amaretto
4 eggs, separated, plus 1 egg white
for sprinkling
tablespoons unbleached all-purpose flour
1 cup milk
pinch of cream of tartar (optional)
confectioners' sugar, for decorating

SERVES 6

40

1 Preheat the oven to 400°F. Butter a 6-cup soufflé dish and sprinkle with superfine sugar. Sprinkle the cookies with 2 tablespoons of the Amaretto and set aside.

2 Mix the 4 egg yolks with 2 tablespoons of the superfine sugar and the flour. Stir until smooth. Put the milk in a heavy saucepan and bring it just to a boil. Remove from the heat and gradually add the hot milk to the beaten egg mixture, stirring.

3 Pour the milk and egg mixture back into the pan. Set it over medium-low heat and simmer gently for 4 minutes or until thickened, stirring constantly. Add the remaining Amaretto and remove the pan from the heat.

4 In a scrupulously clean, grease-free bowl, whisk the 5 egg whites until they form soft peaks. (If not using a copper bowl, add the cream of tartar as soon as the whites are frothy.) Add the remaining sugar and continue whisking until stiff.

5 Add about one-quarter of the whites to the Amaretto mixture and stir in with a rubber spatula. Add the remaining whites and fold in gently.

6 Spoon half the mixture into the prepared dish. Cover with a layer of the moistened amaretti cookies, then spoon the remaining soufflé mixture evenly on the top.

7 Bake the dish for 20 minutes in the preheated oven, or until the soufflé is risen and lightly browned on top. Sprinkle with sifted confectioners' sugar and serve immediately.

Hot Desserts

Cherry Pudding

INGREDIENTS

1 pound ripe cherries
2 tablespoons kirsch or fruit brandy or
1 tablespoon lemon juice
1 tablespoon confectioners' sugar
3 tablespoons unbleached all-purpose flour
3 tablespoons granulated sugar
¾ cup milk or cream
2 eggs
grated zest of ½ lemon
pinch of freshly grated nutmeg
¼ teaspoon vanilla extract

SERVES 4

1 Pit the ripe cherries. Combine them in a mixing bowl with the kirsch, fruit brandy or lemon juice and confectioners' sugar. Set aside for about 1–2 hours.

2 Preheat the oven to 375°F. Generously butter an 10-inch oval gratin dish or other shallow heat proof dish.

3 Sift the flour into a bowl. Add the sugar. Slowly whisk in the milk until smoothly blended. Add the eggs, lemon zest, nutmeg and vanilla extract and whisk until well combined and smooth.

4 Scatter the cherries evenly in the baking dish. Pour on the batter and bake in the preheated oven for 45 minutes, or until the pudding is set and puffed

around the edges; it is ready when a knife inserted in the center comes out clean. Serve either warm or at room temperature.

43

Chocolate, Date & Walnut Pudding

44

INGREDIENTS

2 tablespoons chopped walnuts
2 tablespoons chopped dates
2 eggs
1 teaspoon vanilla extract
2 tablespoons superfine sugar
3 tablespoons whole wheat flour
1 tablespoon unsweetened cocoa powder
2 tablespoons milk

SERVES 4

1 First, grease a 5-cup heat proof baking dish or mixing bowl and place a small circle of baking parchment paper or wax paper in the bottom. Spoon in all the chopped walnuts and dates. Preheat the oven to 350°F.

2 Separate the eggs and place the yolks in a mixing bowl with the vanilla extract and sugar. Place the bowl over a pan of hot water and whisk until the mixture is thick and pale.

3 Sift the flour and cocoa into the mixture and fold them in lightly. Stir in the milk, to moisten the mixture slightly. Whisk the egg whites until they hold soft peaks and fold them in.

4 Spoon the mixture into the basin and bake for 40–45 minutes, or until risen and firm to the touch. Serve immediately.

Creole Bread & Butter Pudding

INGREDIENTS

4 dried apricots, chopped
1 tablespoon raisins
2 tablespoons golden raisins
1 tablespoon chopped candied citrus peel
1 loaf French bread, thinly sliced
4 tablespoons butter, melted
½ cup superfine sugar
3 eggs
½ teaspoon vanilla extract
2 cups milk
⅔ cup heavy or whipping cream
2 tablespoons rum
SAUCE
⅔ cup heavy or whipping cream
2 tablespoons plain yogurt
1–2 tablespoons rum
1 tablespoon superfine sugar

SERVES 4–6

2 Whisk together the sugar, eggs and vanilla extract. Heat the milk and cream until just boiling and whisk into the eggs. Strain over the bread and fruit. Sprinkle the rum on top. Press the bread down, cover with foil and leave for 20 minutes.

1 Preheat the oven to 350°F. Lightly butter a deep 6-cup heat proof baking dish. Mix the dried fruits with the mixed peel and sprinkle a little in the dish. Brush both sides of the bread slices with melted butter. Fill the dish with alternate layers of bread and dried fruit, finishing with a layer of bread.

3 Bake in a roasting pan half filled with boiling water for 1 hour or until the custard is set. Remove the foil and cook for 10 minutes more, until golden.

4 Warm all the sauce ingredients together in a small pan, stirring gently. Serve alongside the hot pudding.

Blackberry Cobbler

INGREDIENTS

6 cups blackberries
1 cup superfine sugar
3 tablespoons unbleached all-purpose flour
grated zest of 1 lemon
2 tablespoons sugar mixed with
¼ teaspoon grated nutmeg
TOPPING
2 cups unbleached all-purpose flour
1 cup superfine sugar
1 tablespoon baking powder
¼ teaspoon salt
1 cup milk
½ cup butter, melted

SERVES 8

46

1 First preheat the oven to 350°F. In a mixing bowl, combine all the blackberries with the superfine sugar, flour and lemon zest. Stir gently to blend together before transferring to a 10-cup heat proof baking dish.

2 To make the topping, sift the flour, sugar, baking powder, and salt into a large bowl. Set aside. Combine the milk and butter in a large measuring cup.

3 Gradually stir the butter and milk mixture into the dry ingredients in the bowl and stir with a wooden spoon until the batter becomes smooth.

4 Spoon the batter over the fruit mixture, spreading it right to the edges. Sprinkle with the sugar and nutmeg mixture, then bake in the preheated oven for about 50 minutes, until the topping is set and lightly browned. Serve hot.

Apple Soufflé Omelette

48

1 For the filling, gently sauté the apple slices in the butter and sugar until just tender. Stir in the cream and keep warm while you make the omelette.

2 Place the egg yolks in a bowl with the cream and sugar and beat well. Whisk the egg whites until stiff, then fold into the yolk mixture.

3 Melt the butter in a large heavy frying pan and pour in the soufflé mixture, spreading it evenly. Cook for 1 minute until golden underneath, then place under a hot broiler and brown the top.

4 Slide the omelette onto a plate, top with the apple filling, then fold the omelette in half. Sift confectioners' sugar liberally over the omelette, and serve immediately.

INGREDIENTS

4 eggs, separated
2 tablespoons cream
1 tablespoon superfine sugar .
1 tablespoon butter
confectioners' sugar, to decorate
FILLING
1 Granny Smith apple, peeled, cored and sliced
2 tablespoons butter
2 tablespoons light brown sugar
3 tablespoons cream

SERVES 2

COOK'S TIP
For a summer variation, use fresh raspberries or strawberries instead of apples.

Plum Filo Pockets

INGREDIENTS

½ cup ricotta cheese
1 tablespoon raw sugar
½ teaspoon ground cloves
8 large firm plums, halved and pitted
8 sheets filo pastry
sunflower oil, for brushing
confectioners' sugar, to decorate

SERVES 4

1 First, preheat the oven to 425°F and then combine the ricotta cheese, raw sugar and ground cloves in a small bowl. Stir well until combined.

2 Sandwich the plum halves back together with a spoonful of the cheese mixture. Cut the filo sheets into 16 pieces, about 9 inches square. Brush one lightly with oil and place a second on top diagonally. Repeat with the other squares.

3 Put a plum on each square and wrap the pastry around it, pinching the corners together. Bake for 15–18 minutes until golden. Dust with confectioners' sugar.

49

Fruity Bread Pudding

2 Quickly remove the pan from the heat and carefully stir in the bread, spices and sliced banana. Mix well. Spoon this mixture into a shallow 5-cup heat proof baking dish. Then pour the milk evenly over the top of the mixture.

3 Sprinkle the top with the raw sugar and bake 25–30 minutes, until it is set and golden brown. Serve hot or cold, with yogurt.

INGREDIENTS

½ cup mixed dried fruit
⅔ cup apple juice
4 ounces stale whole wheat or white bread, diced
1 teaspoon pumpkin pie spice
1 large banana, sliced
⅔ cup milk
1 tablespoon raw sugar
plain yogurt, to serve

SERVES 4

1 Preheat the oven to 400°F. Place the dried fruit in a saucepan with the apple juice and bring to a boil.

COOK'S TIP

Different types of bread and their degree of staleness will cause variation in the amount of liquid absorbed, so you may need to adjust the amount of milk to allow for this.

Gingerbread Upside-Down Pudding

INGREDIENTS

1 tablespoon light brown sugar
4 peaches, halved and pitted, or 8 canned
peach halves
8 walnut halves
yogurt or whipped cream, to serve
BASE
1 cup whole wheat flour
1½ teaspoons ground ginger
½ teaspoon baking soda
1 teaspoon ground cinnamon
½ cup dark brown sugar
1 egg
½ cup milk
¼ cup sunflower oil

SERVES 4–6

1 First, preheat the oven to 350°F and brush the bottom and sides of a 9-inch round springform pan with oil. Sprinkle the sugar over the bottom.

2 Arrange the peach halves, cut-side down, in the pan with a walnut half in each.

3 Make the base. Sift together the flour, ginger, baking soda, and cinnamon, then stir in the sugar. Beat together the egg, milk and oil, then mix into the dry ingredients until smooth.

4 Pour the mixture evenly over the peaches and bake for 35–40 minutes, until firm to the touch. Release onto a serving plate. Serve hot with yogurt or whipped cream.

51

Chocolate
Desserts

French Chocolate Cake

INGREDIENTS

1 cup unsalted butter, cut into pieces
9 ounces good-quality semisweet chocolate,
chopped
½ cup granulated sugar
2 tablespoons brandy or orange-flavor liqueur
5 eggs
1 tablespoon unbleached all-purpose flour
confectioners' sugar, to decorate
sour cream and fresh cherries, to serve

SERVES 10

1 Preheat the oven to 350°F. Line the bottom of a 9-inch springform pan with a circle of baking parchment. Wrap foil around the pan so it is water-tight.

2 Stir the butter, chocolate and granulated sugar over low heat until smooth. Cool slightly. Stir in the liqueur. In a bowl, beat the eggs lightly, then beat in the flour. Slowly beat in the chocolate mixture to blend. Pour into the pan. Smooth the surface.

3 Place the springform pan in a roasting pan. Fill the roasting pan with enough boiling water to come ¾ inch up the side of the springform pan. Bake for 25–30 minutes, until the edge of the cake is set, but the center is still soft. Remove the foil. Cool in the pan on a wire rack (the cake will sink and may crack).

4 Turn the cake upside-down onto a wire rack. Release the springform pan and remove the paper. The bottom of the cake is now the top.

5 Cut 6–8 strips of baking parchment 1 inch wide and place them randomly over the cake, or make a lattice-style pattern if you wish. Dust the cake with confectioners' sugar, then carefully remove the paper. Slide the cake onto a serving plate and serve with sour cream and fresh cherries.

White Chocolate Cheesecake

INGREDIENTS

5 ounces (about 16-18) graham crackers
½ cup blanched hazelnuts, toasted
4 tablespoons unsalted butter, melted
½ teaspoon ground cinnamon
FILLING
12 ounces good quality white chocolate, chopped
½ cup heavy or whipping cream
3 packages (8 ounces each) cream cheese, softened
¼ cup granulated sugar
4 eggs
1 tablespoon vanilla extract
TOPPING
2 cups sour cream
¼ cup granulated sugar
1 tablespoon hazelnut-flavor liqueur or 1 tea-
spoon vanilla extract
white chocolate curls, to decorate
unsweetened cocoa powder, for dusting (optional)

SERVES 16–20

1 Preheat the oven to 350°F and grease a 9-inch springform pan. Process the graham crackers and hazelnuts to fine crumbs, then mix with the butter and cinnamon. Press the mixture onto the bottom and sides of the pan and bake for 5–7 minutes, or until just set.

2 Lower the oven to 300°F. Make the filling. Melt the chocolate and cream over low heat until smooth, stirring frequently. Cool.

3 Beat the cream cheese and sugar until smooth; beat in the eggs, one at a time, the white chocolate mixture and the vanilla. Pour into the baked crust and bake for 45–55 minutes, or until the edge of the filling is firm but the center is still slightly soft. Transfer to a wire rack, still in the pan, and increase the oven temperature to 400°F.

4 Make the topping. Whisk the sour cream with the sugar and vanilla and pour it over the cheesecake, spreading it evenly. Return the cheesecake to the oven for 5–7 minutes. Turn off the oven, but do not open the door for 1 hour.

5 Transfer the cheesecake to a wire rack to cool in the pan. Remove the pan, then chill the cheesecake, loosely covered, overnight.

6 Place the cheesecake on a serving plate. Decorate the top with chocolate curls and dust lightly with cocoa, if desired.

Chocolate Pavlova with Chocolate Curls

INGREDIENTS

2½ cups confectioners' sugar
1 tablespoon unsweetened cocoa powder
1 teaspoon cornstarch
5 egg whites, at room temperature
pinch of salt
1 teaspoon cider vinegar or lemon juice
CHOCOLATE CREAM
6 ounces good quality semisweet chocolate,
chopped
½ cup milk
2 tablespoons butter, cut into pieces
2 tablespoons brandy
2 cups heavy or whipping cream
TOPPING
4 cups mixed berries or diced mango, papaya,
lychees and pineapple
chocolate curls
confectioners' sugar

SERVES 8–10

1 Preheat the oven to 325°F. Place a sheet of baking parchment onto a baking sheet and mark an 8-inch circle on it. Sift 3 tablespoons of the confectioners' sugar with the cocoa and cornstarch and set aside. Using an electric mixer, beat the egg whites until frothy. Add the salt and beat until the whites form stiff peaks.

2 Sprinkle the remaining confectioners' sugar into the egg whites, a little at a time, making sure each addition is blended in before beating in the next. Fold in the cornstarch mixture, then quickly fold in the vinegar or lemon juice.

3 Now spoon the mixture onto the paper circle, with the sides higher than the center. Bake for 1 hour, until set, then turn off the oven but leave the meringue inside for 1 hour longer. Remove from the oven, peel off the paper and let cool.

4 Make the chocolate cream. Melt the chocolate in the milk over low heat, stirring until smooth. Remove from the heat and whisk in the butter and brandy. Cool for 1 hour.

5 Transfer the meringue to a serving plate. When the chocolate mixture has cooled, but is not too firm, beat the cream until soft peaks form. Stir half the cream into the chocolate mixture to lighten it, then fold in the remaining cream. Spoon it into the center of the meringue. Arrange fruit and chocolate curls in the center of the meringue, on top of the cream. Dust with confectioners' sugar and serve.

56

Chocolate Cream Puffs

INGREDIENTS

1 cup water
½ teaspoon salt
1 tablespoon granulated sugar
½ cup unsalted butter, cut into pieces
¼ cups unbleached all-purpose flour, sifted
2 tablespoons unsweetened cocoa powder, sifted
4–5 eggs
1 recipe Chocolate Cream (page 62),
for filling
GLAZE
1¼ cups heavy or whipping cream
4 tablespoons unsalted butter, cut into pieces
1 tablespoon corn syrup
8 ounces good quality bittersweet chocolate,
chopped
1 teaspoon vanilla extract

MAKES 12

1 Preheat the oven to 425°F. Grease a baking sheet. Bring the water, salt, sugar and butter to a boil. Remove from the heat; add the flour and cocoa. Stir vigorously until the mixture pulls away from the sides of the pan. Heat for 1 minute, beating constantly. Remove from the heat.

2 Beat in four of the eggs, one at a time. The mixture should be thick, smooth and shiny and fall from a spoon. If it is too dry, beat the fifth egg separately, then add it to the mixture gradually. Spoon the batter into an icing bag with a star tip and pipe 12 puffs on the baking sheet.

3 Bake the puffs for 35–40 minutes until puffed and golden. Slice off the top third of each puff and return both tops and bottoms, cut side up, to the baking sheet. Return them to the oven for a few more minutes. Cool on a wire rack.

4 Spoon the chocolate cream into a piping bag fitted with a plain tip. Fill the bottom of each puff, then cover with a top.

5 Make the glaze. Melt the cream, butter, syrup, chocolate and vanilla until smooth, stirring often. Remove from the heat and let cool for about 20–30 minutes, until slightly thickened. Pour a little glaze over each of the cream puffs, or dip the top of each puff into the glaze, and let set. To serve, arrange the puffs on a serving plate in a single layer or pile them up on top of each other.

Chocolate Loaf with Coffee Sauce

INGREDIENTS

6 ounces good quality semisweet chocolate,
chopped
4 tablespoons butter, softened
4 large eggs, separated
2 tablespoons rum or brandy (optional)
pinch of cream of tartar
chocolate curls and chocolate-covered
coffee beans, to decorate
COFFEE SAUCE
2½ cups milk
9 egg yolks
¼ cup superfine sugar
1 teaspoon vanilla extract
1 tablespoon instant coffee powder, dissolved
in 2 tablespoons hot water

SERVES 6–8

60

1 Line a 5-cup loaf pan with plastic wrap. Place the semisweet chocolate in a bowl placed over hot water and leave for 3–5 minutes, then stir.

2 Remove the bowl from the pan and quickly beat in the butter, egg yolks, one at a time, and rum or brandy, if using.

3 In a clean grease-free bowl, using an electric mixer, beat the egg whites slowly until frothy. Add the cream of tartar, increase the speed and continue beating until they form stiff peaks. Stir one-third of the egg whites into the chocolate mixture, then fold in the remaining whites. Pour into the lined loaf pan and smooth the top. Cover and freeze for 2–3 hours, until set.

4 Make the coffee sauce. Bring the milk to a simmer over medium heat. Whisk together the egg yolks and the superfine sugar for 2–3 minutes until thick and creamy, then whisk in the hot milk and return the mixture to the saucepan. With a wooden spoon, stir over low heat until the sauce begins to thicken and coat the back of the spoon. Strain the custard into a chilled bowl, stir in the vanilla extract and coffee and set aside to cool, stirring occasionally. Chill.

5 To serve, uncover the loaf pan and dip the bottom into hot water for 10 seconds. Invert the chocolate loaf onto a board and peel off the plastic wrap. Cut the loaf into slices and serve topped with the coffee sauce. Decorate with the chocolate curls and chocolate-covered coffee beans.

Hazelnut Meringue Torte with Pears

INGREDIENTS

¾ cup granulated sugar
1 vanilla pod, split
2 cups water
4 ripe pears, peeled, halved and cored
6 egg whites
2½ cups confectioners' sugar
1¼ cups ground hazelnuts
1 teaspoon vanilla extract
*2 ounces good quality semisweet chocolate,
melted*
chocolate caraque, to decorate
CHOCOLATE CREAM
2 cups whipping cream
*10 ounces good-quality semisweet chocolate,
melted*
4 tablespoons hazelnut-flavor liqueur

SERVES 8–10

1 In a pan large enough to hold the pears in a single layer, combine the sugar, vanilla pod and water. Bring to a boil, stirring until the sugar dissolves. Reduce the heat and add the pears. Cover and simmer for 12–15 minutes until tender. Remove from heat and let cool. Preheat the oven to 350°F.

2 Draw a 9-inch circle on two sheets of baking parchment and place on two baking sheets.

3 Whisk the egg whites until soft peaks form, then gradually add the confectioners' sugar, whisking until stiff and glossy. Gently fold in the nuts and vanilla and spoon the meringue onto the marked circles. Bake for 1 hour. Turn off the heat and cool in the oven.

4 Slice the pear halves lengthwise. Then, make the chocolate cream. Beat the cream into soft peaks, then fold in the melted chocolate and liqueur. Put a third of the chocolate cream into an icing bag fitted with a star tip. Spread one meringue layer with half the remaining chocolate cream and top with half the pears. Pipe rosettes around the edge.

5 Top with the second meringue and the remaining chocolate cream and pear slices. Pipe rosettes around the edge. Drizzle the melted chocolate over the pears and decorate with the chocolate shavings. Chill for 1 hour before serving.

Index